BLOSSOM AND BONE

NICOLE LYONS

SUDDEN DENOUEMENT
PUBLISHING

Blossom and Bone
Copyright © 2018 by Nicole Lyons.

Published in the United States of America by
Sudden Denouement Publishers

SUDDEN DENOUEMENT
PUBLISHING

ISBN 9780999079683
Library of Congress Control Number: 2018956088

Editor: Christine E. Ray
Cover Design: Mitch Green
Typesetting & Layout: Mitch Green

PRAISE FOR BLOSSOM AND BONE

"A beautifully crafted work of art that will punch you in the face with its gritty realism before soothing your wounds with elegant prose, thought provoking lines, and sublime imagery."
– Samuel Decker Thompson, author of Our Fucked Up Hearts

"Lyons is connecting on a primal level here, all the while brilliantly splitting herself along dual lines. She draws an effortless parallel between desire to live and acceptance she cannot beat death."
– Nicholas Gagnier, author of Leonard The Liar

"I knew from the first page that Blossom and Bone would rekindle the love affair I had with 'HUSH' and 'I am a World of Uncertainties Disguised as a Girl'. Lyons words lasso and then cajole your heart. Old or new fan, you will love how she rips you apart, and then puts you back together again. This poetry book needs to be on your bedside table, because I promise you, you will reach for it again and again."
- Alfa Holden, author of Abandoned Breaths

"Nicole Lyons is a writer of the now. She is a woman of the now. Her pulse can be heard in every syllable in Blossom and Bone. There is a kindling rage in her words, a don't-you-dare-turn-away quality to the exorcism of her truths, she stares into places others skip over, she disgorges the dirt like an excavator of pain, and presents it as you would a film, blinking in front of you, refusing to let you ignore it."
– Candice Louisa Daquin, author of Pinch The Lock

TABLE OF CONTENTS

For Ashley,
who has always been
the thorn in my side
and the rose in my heart.

FOREWORD

Have you ever read an author you feel an intuitive bond with? That their words take on a life of their own, not separate from, but part of the magnetic energy of that author and you realize you have made an investment in a person you have never even met? If you have experienced this feeling you are probably a lover of books and you may have quite a few authors whom you would categorize thus. No matter how much time passes, even if you have not read a book of theirs recently, if someone asks you to name your most influential authors you will find yourself bringing them up as if they were a family member.

Because like music, we feel such a passion and thus, a fierce connection to, people we may not personally know but whose minds, sound, language and art moves us in ways we cannot even express, and respond to almost unconsciously. I compare this to falling in love, why do we fall in love with one person versus all the others we meet in our huge world? Can we really know the answer? And yet there is it, a magnetic pull that secures our investment to that person, often for a very long time. Perhaps this is what sets us apart from other animals, we respond with our senses and our minds, our hearts and our souls, there is so much that goes into why a person moves us and how much this impacts our life.

For those who are unaccustomed to feeling this about a writer, welcome to the world of book addicts, where we hoard our favorite authors like our last chocolate. Nicole Lyons has generated this kind of following, she is already in her own right, a cult, for something in her writing persuades or compels people to believe in her, and feel an intense connection with her craft. That doesn't happen to every writer, and when it does, sometimes fame and fortune play a role, but in Nicole's case her work is the reason she is so beloved, she literally spills

9

herself onto the page and those who like what they see, stay for the long haul.

Consequently Nicole Lyons has amassed a serious following online even before the sales success of her first two collections of poetry that were both best sellers on Amazon, no small feat for any author. It wasn't her marketing alacrity that caused this sensation, it was the immediate response from readers, who could through her work, find something to hold onto and claim for themselves. Above all else, this tells you a little of the kind of person Nicole Lyons is and the kind of work she produces, even before you have read her, you know there is something special about this girl.

How does any writer in today's saturated market, set themselves apart and stand out? Too often the methods employed are glaringly obvious or nepotistic and thus, have less natural formation than a writer whose sheer soulfulness and sublime control over words, position them at the head of the crowd. When you read a poem by Nicole you know it's by her, she leaves you in no doubt of who she is, and what she's here to do. She's here to tell you how it is, and not let you nod your head and say 'yeah I know that already' because you don't know it until you've read her. That's because she owns her own brand of language, literally.

For myself, being asked to write a foreword on this savage and lovely collection of poems, it became apparent I had entered the cult of Nicole quite a long time ago when I first began reading her. Her poems got under my skin, they were unapologetic and raw, they begged me to not turn away, and they stayed with me after I put the book down. All my life I have been attracted to authors who possessed this bewitchment and too often, writers I found in bookstores fell short by trying too hard or simply not having the magic necessary. Nicole is a real, breathing living creature, she's in her books not just the author of her books, her life, her suffering and her survival drip from the pages, she doesn't present a safe and neatly tied bow of a book she gives you her everything and just as she does, she leaves a little back so you want more.

You know when an author has inked themselves to you, because you find yourself suggesting their work to others, not based on category, 'oh you like poetry? Well then you should read …' but almost as a prescriptive. I would give Nicole Lyons' work as a prescription to anyone seeking truth in their world. I would throw away medications and ask someone to read Nicole in lieu of therapy, or an honest conversation. If you have been in a dark place, if you are still there, or you know what it feels like, if you have survived and grown wings, if you loved someone who experienced this, if you can empathize with the world's ills, then her work will speak to you. Probably even if you hadn't any of the above, you'd get something out of Nicole's work because she doesn't let anyone off the hook. Her work grabs you by the throat and demands a serious audience. Because of this, she's unforgettable.

I'm honored to recommend Nicole Lyons' third book of poetry, Blossom and Bone to all of you who already love her and follow her and those of you who have yet to. In this collection you will find the heart of an incredible woman, who appears to have lived many lifetimes in one, and has that eerie second-sight of any natural wordsmith. Nicole's work is a permanent fixture in my reading experience, that's the kind of impact she makes, and beyond that, she leaves you with many thoughts on the fragility of this world, but ultimately a consideration of its redemptive abilities through the power of love.

- Candice Louisa Daquin, Author of Pinch The Lock

Find more of Candice's work at thefeatheredsleep.com

ONCE UPON A TIME

I am standing here, screaming,
"I live, I live. I love."
and they are laughing as you dig in
to this pile of bullshit,
shovels full of our own wasted lives.
Oh, if we all could live,
right and good like stories
filled with mighty conquests
and happier endings.
My feet are covered in this waste,
wishes treading the water
that has been pissed out of finer souls
than we could ever hope to be.
We should hope less and dig more,
there are treasures to be found
beneath the pile of golden souls
who would think well enough
to shit outside the gates of their own
once upon a time.

DESPAIR

Despair, my coldest
lost lover has returned
to pull my warmth,
and cast his shadow
over me.

BRING YOUR WISHES

It is empty in here.
This place that once
felt the fire of falling stars
is now cold in my fading light.
So I shall invite you in
and ask you to bring your wishes,
and perhaps the both of us
will burst like suns again.

MY EASY HEART

I have always loved the cold
dark places where feelings go
to hide, as I have loved something
about the easy way my heart
shatters the second it rubs
up against something warm.

THE KEEPER OF TIME

I swear to God, I am not proud of it,
this wishing and unwishing,
how I keep wishing and unwishing for more,
as if that could make nothing become something,
or turn something back into nothing,
or take them all away, and leave me with maybe.
This wishing and unwishing is killing me.

If I could go back and take it all back,
or change it all I would, God help me, I would.
There are so many things I would change
and so many things I couldn't, and wouldn't,
and would never want to, but if I started
to change one thing, I would never stop.

I would wish to be the keeper of time, to whisper
my secrets to you, and we would sit beyond time
together and I would tell you that you can
change this because I have kept your time.
I have kept your seconds, your wishes,
your memories and your love, here,
in this notebook, and I give it back to you
now with an eraser and a pencil.

And we would look there, on your notebook,
on its dog-eared edges and its faded cover,
and you would wish for brighter colours and
I would tell you to open the book of your life,
read the notebook of your time,
because I am giving it back to you.

I am giving you this one pass, this one time,
as the keeper of your time, the keeper of your sins,
I give them all back to you.

I give you back your dreams, rewrite them.
Write them all, and don't write them
as if you were afraid of what people would think.
Don't write them as if you haven't been
given a second chance upon a first chance,
because you haven't, but still,
write them without fear, without consequence,
without any measure of hope or of sorrow,
I ask you to write, so write now.
I can not reset time,
I can not make things right
as you see them be,
because your right is wrong
in everyone else's eyes,
in cosmic eyes that stare down at us all.

Don't read the rewrite,
and I will keep you secretly,
and give you this page and this pencil to write
all of the things you wanted to write,
all of the things you wanted to keep,
all of the things you wanted to change,
all of the things that are time and are not,
and will not or never be,
and I ask you to write it solidly,
without despair, without guilt, without question.

Write the rewrite that I can never grant you,
and sign your name to the bottom of it, proudly.
For there is nothing wrong with a rewrite,
in this life or in others, there is nothing wrong
with wanting a rewrite, even if we love
our stories and the way they began
with a once upon a time and ended
with a happily ever after,
because you are many stories.
You are a great book of love, and loss, and light,
and the wisdom of your pages, between your pages
could never be rewritten into words greater
than any of your stories I have already read.

WIPING YOUR LIGHT

There is something in you
I am unable to reach,
but I feel it, I feel you.
I feel your pain,
and I see your light, spilling
from cupped palms placed
at the foot of unworthy altars.
And try as I might, I stretch
and I twist to reach you,
to empty your hands
of that brilliant pain,
but each time I twist
I come up empty-handed,
and wiping your light
from the corners of my mouth.

SHAME

Shame, my loneliest
lost lover has returned
to take his comfort,
in the sanctuary of my bones.

MOSTLY DEAD ONES

You with the goddess heart
and that cemetery soul,
of course, you are a dragon now.
Every ghost you have ever loved
has salted your earth
with their coming
and with their going, again.
Breathe, woman, breathe!
Wrath and fire will shoo the dead
from their place of rest
and you will cultivate love once again.

CRUSHED WET WILDFLOWERS

She tasted like wildflowers;
crushed, wet wildflowers
carried in sticky palms
through farmers' fields,
just before dawn.

IN DAISIES

Come, let's follow the sun
while she chases the moon,
and I will cover your bruises
in daisies.

I WON'T ALWAYS BE ME

I won't always walk gently.
Sometimes I will stomp,
and I will rage,
and my footsteps will shake
the mountains of love
you have heaped upon my earth.
I won't always speak kindly.
Sometimes I will spit,
and I will scream,
and the venom from my tongue
will poison the oceans of love
you have brought to my shores.
I won't always live passionately.
Sometimes I will hide,
and I will cry,
and the blackness from my soul
will darken the gardens of love
you have planted at my door.
I won't always be me.
Sometimes I will be the very thing
I have been fighting against,
and it will swallow me,
and it will laugh,
and I will climb out of the depths
of it all to meet you gently,
and kindly, and passionately again.

THAT ONE SUMMER

I had yet to feel your sweat on my neck,
but I knew I loved you already.
Like red roses pulling yellow leaves,
and green thumbs dipped in sugar,
I loved you sweetly.
Like desperate phone calls made
to lonely operators in the middle
of the night, just this side of the beach,
I loved you urgently.
You were my lime green popsicle and the reason
I learned how to fake a cough that summer,
and why I timed it to land perfectly
between the fighting upstairs
and the whistling on the tracks outside.
I coughed, and I flushed, and then I ran,
to you, waiting under orange lights
and humming songs about fallen angels,
and my God, how I loved you.

CHICKEN DINNER

We crossed that bridge
the second you came upon it,
beach blankets soaked
and the lovers' notes
carved a generation before us
had seemed entirely too heavy
until that night when I sat down
to undercooked chicken and overcooked rice
served with an unconditional side of love.

I remember feeling sorry for the chicken
at that moment in all of my wise teenage years,
and having an epiphany right there
at the dinner table next to an alcoholic
control freak who called me stepdaughter
and walked upon me to seal it
like the gummy flap of an envelope
stuffed with unloved letters,
and a mother who wore exhaustion
hidden inside her navy pumps.

Death, no matter how it is served
will always precede dinner
unless breakfast beats it to lunch.

I thought of myself as quite wise
beyond my years in that moment,
still warm from the glow
of your summer love and giddy
because you and the chicken
filled the pit in my stomach
that always seemed to pound

when he cleared his throat.
And when I heard him gag
behind the ball of his fist and blame it
on the weather and too big a gulp,
I almost didn't wish he would choke
on chicken or the spite hidden beneath it.

UNDER YOUR BED

I have loved as I have never been loved,
and in loving as I have never been,
I have held the hands of gods
and laid weeping before the closed fists
of disappointment dripping with my own blood
and barely skimming forgiveness.
Perhaps it will come to me,
this love, a love, beneath your bed,
behind the curtains or under you mother
and her Sunday night dinner,
the one I was invited to
before the devil tickled my back
and your angels scorched my belly.
I wear these marks well,
my kisses from heaven
and my brushes with hell,
yet here I am on my knees again,
looking for the love you dropped under your bed.
I know it's here somewhere,
amongst the monsters and the memories,
making friends with the lonely socks
missing their mates, and reaching
inside the crumpled wrappers,
the pink ones that burst the stars
upon your tongue before he broke the door down
and taught you all the ways you should never love.

MELANCHOLY

Melancholy, my longest
lost lover has returned,
to dance with me, again.

ROBBING AIR

I don't want to live this life anymore,
but you are pinks and deep hues,
the tangerine clouds behind sunsets
that giggle and puff themselves
into the shape of my mother,
when she slouched proudly
against the cupboards that robbed my air.
You are the pink of her that opened
the doors on their mothers
getting busy with our uncles,
and the red screeching from a pillowcase
bursting with the Siamese kittens they drowned.
You are deep hues and an ugly reminder
of small towns and smaller minds,
stroked once and cut twice
from a life, we are all running from.

NICOLE LYONS

DROPPING LEAVES OF DREAMS

A family tree stands,
a great willow.
Rippled branches stretching thick,
reaching the grandest heights
to obscure the sun
and steal the light.

A family tree boasts,
a great willow.
Shooting suckers along hills,
claiming dominance
over pretty paths
long ago deserted.

A family tree sways,
a great willow.
Shooing the crows that perch,
and shading
the birches that dare
grow too close.

A family tree weeps,
a great willow.
Dropping leaves, of dreams
and unhappy children
who would swing
from its branches.

UNDER THE SYCAMORE

I carved my place in this world,
into the bark of a beautiful
old sycamore tree
long before I cut my teeth
on the boys who would bend
her branches.
My place was crooked
and she was hesitant,
shedding me off in big chunks
quicker than I could pierce her
flesh, but I was forceful,
and she relented.

I was young and untouchable.
Air thinning, mind spinning,
I inhaled freedom
in the muggy summer
sun, and exhaled secrets.
Spewing my soul under a canopy
of hushed greens
and swallows singing.

I hung my hopes
from her branches,
and she, catching sun,
cast stained glass
colours along my pure,
bronzed skin.

I found my peace
on mossy ground,
legs stretched, painted
pink toes tracing
the strong lines of her
supple trunk.
I spent days, like that.
Daydreaming of first kisses
and a love I didn't understand.

I watched her fall.
Reaching tips to dying suns
as she spilled my secrets
into grey skies.
Casting shadows
upon my thirteenth year,
and the dreams she had
dropped at my feet.

I blossomed in the spring,
without her. Alone but for
the gnarled limbs
like burned branches
that carved their place
in this world, into me,
long before I cut my teeth
on the boys who would
never bend my branches.

His place was sacred
and mine. I fought,
ripping chunks of meat
quicker than he could pierce
my flesh, but he was forceful,
and I relented.

I TOLD HIM NO

He told me how brave I was,
writing my story into a sea of stigma,
how my words, my voice,
would break waves and save souls,
a lighthouse for the mentally ill,
the distraught, the unloved.
I told him no.

He told me how beautiful I was,
smiling sadly with eyes like burnt moons
hiding secrets behind the sun,
a gravitational pull for the mentally ill,
the distraught, the unloved.
I told him no.

He told me how special I was,
tempting great men with good faith,
a harlot born from Satan's tongue,
a perfect delusion for the mentally ill,
the distraught, the unloved.
I told him no.

He told me he was mentally ill,
distraught, unloved,
in dire need of desperate release,
and salvation would only come on his knees,
shaking to the sound of my voice.
I told him no.

He told me how sorry I would be
when he twisted my words like arms
and shot arrows through the bull's-eye
he had painted on my chest.
I told him no.

I am not the voice of a saviour,
nor the hint of a wish,
I am fucking dangerous,
coming to claw the truth
from behind a liar's lips.

NOTHING TO SAY

There is nothing to be said
about the way you hover over me,
nothing about the way you grind
your hips and your filth against me
from somewhere inside of places,
I have never been.
There is nothing to be said
about the way you breathe,
hot and filled with rage,
against the back of my neck
when I write your ugly truths
into existence and speak
my words above yours.
There is something to be said
about the way a woman's voice
carries, her soul across oceans,
lifts her power over mountains,
charges her truth through wastelands,
gaining speed and strength
from every ear it cradles.
But there is nothing to be said
about the shoulders too weak
to hold the weight of her voice,
the ears too ignorant to listen,
and the mouths too vile to spit
anything other than hate.
No, there is nothing much to say
about any of that, but you can
be damn sure I am going to say it.

YOU'RE DEAD TO ME

And now I shall bury you,
remembering you as if
you had only been seasons.

REGRET

Regret, my wistful
lost lover has returned
to torment me, churning
riptides through my veins
to breach my heartbreak
and flood his madness
into my soul.

HER BELT

I wonder if she thought of me
when she cinched her belt,
and if she had to punch
extra holes in the leather
before she did it,
and if it was real leather
or as fake as we were.
I wonder these things,
and quickly follow up
my wondering with more,
like why I am this way,
and if I was the one
who handed her that belt
when I walked into her life
and took it from her.
Living feels hard
when death comes calling,
whispering names
that sound like yours,
but dying seems easy
when life comes calling,
shouting names
that should have been hers.
And maybe that is why
I wonder about that fucking belt
more than anything else.
That belt would have served me better,
holding up the weight of this life
she would have lived
fuller than I have.

LIKE SIN AND SPRING

I wear her name like sin,
wispy and swirling
like the hem of summer
dresses biting the inside
of my thighs.
I wear her moans like spring,
heavy and wet
like coats dripping *why*
down the back of my neck.
I splash in the puddles of her,
the pools of her
like spring and summer,
and I feel the slick wet of them
until I scrunch my toes
against the broken soles
of the hand-me-down shoes
she used to adore.

UNDER MY WING

I have never felt a smooth landing
beneath my feet, nor have I ever
been lucky enough to tuck one under
my wing and breathe great gusts
of relief as if I had been saved.
I know what it's like to scrape myself
and pull away from the concrete
with a mouthful of blood and fear.
I know how that bloody fear tastes
like defeat when I wipe it from my mouth.
I have felt courage, and I know how
it fills my lungs with the taste
of triumph when I get back up and cross
the finish line of every race
I never signed up to run.
I may have never felt a smooth landing
beneath my feet, or ever been lucky
enough to tuck one under my wing,
but I know how it feels to close
my eyes and jump blindly without
anything to save me, but how well I ride
the fall; hard and fast, and always free.

A HARD THING

It is a hard thing, when a mind creeps and wanders,
and everything you want to say comes out
as everything you have sworn you wouldn't.
It is a very hard thing when a mind,
so full and so bright, turns in on itself
and darkness feels like home again.
It is a hard thing when life turns cold
and those who have always kept you warm
have locked you out in freezing rains
to numb yourself to their own numbness.
It is a hard thing to trudge, to keep your mind
and body as whole as splintered can be,
through rapid-fire thoughts of harm and goodbyes.
It is the hardest thing to reach for strange
hands once familiar, to hold and pull hope
from within their warm palms.
It is a hard thing, but it is worth more
than everything in the end.

TELL ME SOMETHING BEAUTIFUL

Tell me how the sunshine felt on your face
after you dropped to your knees and swore
you could no longer go on.
Tell me that the warmth of its rays reached out
to warm the tears from your eyes
and kiss the cries from your lips.
Tell me you found something
beautiful in the breaking,
and when you stood you took it
all away and carried it home with you.
How else could your soul be this golden?
If you hadn't stolen the sun to fill your heart,
and cram your pockets with its pure light.

THIS SIDE OF MIDNIGHT

I believe there is a window,
mounted in mourning, and hung
just this side of midnight.
And when we call out,
through its shattered glass
and torn screens,
something in the universe
shifts, allowing our echoes
and our unfortunate words
to ride the wind, and carry
our secrets into the open
windows of the insomniacs
of the world,
those tragic beasts
that spend their nights
walking with demons,
and wrestling their mental health,
while they wish this world away.
And I think if we whisper,
just a little louder
than library vibes,
or a pitch higher
than the purists that preach
on Sunday morning,
we could spill our secrets
before the clock strikes done,
and someone who has spent
their night wandering
can open the window,
on their side of midnight,
and hear the voices
that never took the time
to walk them home at dawn.

SUNFLOWERS

Do you remember that time
when we sat together,
apart from each other, worlds away?
You asked me if it was okay to lay
your head in my lap and I told you
I would love nothing more than to run
my fingers through your dreams
and talk about when we could
plant our gardens.
And you laid there hot,
and heavy on my thighs
and I told you we should
pick sunflowers and name them all
proudly, this one for love,
this one for her, this one for him,
and this one for them, and for a life
you and I will never ever know.

SOLITUDE

Solitude, my softest
lost lover has returned
to embrace me, to whisper
daydreams down my spine
and sip the poetry from my lips.

COSMIC THINGS

I have fallen in love
with far too many
beautiful things.
Cosmic things,
like the way the sun
shines on dying stars,
and how it eclipses
the wishes of forgotten souls.
I have fallen in love
with the wildest beasts,
the ones that howl
beneath full blue moons,
bursting as they wait to watch
you unbuckle my wishes
from Orion's Belt.
I have fallen in love
with the velvety touch
of the milkiest ways,
and I dread the day when
I wake up and am left
with nothing but the tragic
crash of a love born
only in this world.

TASTING PAIN

I loved him, intensely.
Throat bared, holes in the walls,
sirens wailing, intensely.
But God, did I love him.
I knew we would end
before we had even begun.
But my name was blackened
on his chest and confessions
had been whispered at three a.m.
and I couldn't breathe without him.
And until you have tasted pain
as sweet as his, you can't
begin to understand.

JUST DESSERTS

If only you would vanish and stay
hidden away in some desolate place,
buried and long forgotten,
I wouldn't feel this need to escape
my own mind and the memories
that lurk within.
They enthrall me in the sickest way,
these thoughts upon memories
born out of the torment you fed me.
And sometimes the taste of them,
the regret, surges back into my mouth,
thick like honey, to stick to my tongue.
And I would be lying if I told you
that I didn't think about going back
for a second helping.

DESECRATIONS

I found the pieces
you tried to hide,
buried in secret
places, untouched.
Oh, how I yearn
to lash the beauty
of them and leave
my stain
upon each one.

LOVE BITES

I still pick at these
memories of you.
I pick them
until they bleed.

EVANESCENCE

I swear I was clean before
you came blazing in,
guns firing hot, bursting
into me with pain so sweet
that I begged for a slow death.
But you stole the sweet ache
from my bones and left
the savage bits of you behind,
spraying them all over my world.
They blot out the sun, and leave
me with a forever night.
They crawl over me, inside of me,
and consume me with the filth of memories,
and they whisper about this slow death
and how I should be careful what I wish for.

A SLIP OF HEAVEN

I have seen sinners saved
from bloody knees,
and heard angels sing
from holy things.
But you, my love,
are the bells that ring,
in a heathen's choir
when the devil sings.

MOST DAYS

I don't know if I will ever
know the truth of us,
and what could have been,
what should have been,
what will never be.
But I do know I loved you
and I think you may
have loved me too,
and on most days
that is enough.

MY HEART BREAKING TOMORROW

Today my lips are chapped
from all of the kisses I have
given away, and I can already
feel my heart breaking
again tomorrow.
I have set my soul to repeat
every yesterday when
the vision I held of myself
was still as clear and half
as clean as the hope
I watched you bury
in the earth that smelled
faintly as fresh as my mother
when she used to tell me
how much she loved me
as she scrubbed my hair.
We would laugh when
the strands found their way
beneath her nails
and see-sawed the day away
and her hands clean again.
I smiled when I watched her
pound our garden and her love
into dinner with hands cleaner
than they had any right to be,
and here I am now, pounding love
into supper and scratching
desolate grounds open,
and I watch you bury the leftovers
while I pray for spring rains
to fall and wash it all away,
even though nothing will
ever grow in this place.

A COSMIC DISAPPOINTMENT

I drink
and I scream
and I curse the stars,
and still you are here,
blaring in my fucking veins.

HOPE

Hope, my elusive lost lover
has returned to hang
his worries from my neck
and dig his grave
inside my bones.

IT NEVER HEARD THAT

I don't want to remember exactly
how I was or who I was before you,
and I know that
isn't what this world wants to hear,
but it never listened
to the beat of my broken heart
or caught the pain in my eyes anyway.
It never heard the way I hated myself
when dawn hit my window and sliced
its way through the mountains of maybe
next time I won't hurt myself,
but for now just cut these colours
easy enough to taste something
less bitter than I am.
It never heard that.
It never listened
to the way I could gulp and howl
under the light of a full moon,
a new moon, of any moon,
of a sick and sculpted summer
moon that hung above the grime
I pretended not to notice.
It never heard that.
It never listened
to my voice calling out from the dark
when the last light in me had been dimmed,
it never came to chase the shadows
or the monsters that waited to lunge
the second the lights went out.
It was never there to shine
hope into my darkened heart
or hear the cries of my soiled soul.

It never heard that.
I never knew that silence with you whispered
the most extraordinary tales,
and sitting in the way of sunsets
with you shifted the ugly inside of me,
and burst beautiful rays into the dark of my eyes.
I don't want to remember
who I was when I was without you,
but I do, and I will, and perhaps
remembering how cold it was in the dark
will never let me forget how
I can hear the warmth in the light.

SECOND SUPPER

There is thing in my throat,
I cough and I hack, and I clear
my schedule for every dead-beat dad
and long lost survivor of something
that is offensive right now,
but it still catches;
it still wiggles its way into the muck,
and it sticks here,
right fucking here,
between the roof of my mouth
and the shit apologies I swallowed
yesterday, back in the day,
before I tasted anything
that had been seasoned with honesty.
There is this thing in my throat,
and it swings on the hinges
of my gag reflex, and I gulp
and I breathe, and I swallow it again.
Over and over, I swallow it again,
because it keeps crawling out of my belly
and back up my throat
every fucking time I get used
to the idea of eating anything
other than shame or the ugliness
that has been dished out and served up.
But the sound, that glorious fucking sound,
full of full bodies and their retching
noises I make when swallowing
that shit, is a little more appetizing,
and a hell of a lot more appealing
than the sound of the truth being spit
from my mouth and the creak

of their chairs scraping the floor.
There is this thing in my throat,
and I feed off of it and everyone
and they feed off of me,
and we're all a little fatter now
because of it.

DRAGON SOUL

This life hasn't been easy on me,
I have learned to breathe fire,
and God help any of you
who would ever try
to smother my flames.

SHE IS A STORM

Gently now, wild one,
this world can only
handle so many storms,
and you have
struck this one
with your lightning
and painted the walls of it
with your thunder.
Gently now, wild one,
let them catch their breath.

DESIRE

Desire, my hungriest
lost lover has returned
to consume me.
To set fire to my blood
and stroke his cravings
through my soul.

FROM EVE'S LIPS

I know you think
you want a kiss,
but my tongue
is a serpent,
and my mouth
is a poorly wired cage.

LEGEND

When I was a little girl
they spoke of a legend,
about a wolf and a hunger,
and why I should never wear red,
but the moon pulled the tide
and I was christened a woman,
and the legend was rewritten
when I became the wolf in the end

I KNOW YOU, TOO

I know you know me.
By the ache
in your bones
and the pulse
in your veins,
you know me,
and God help you,
I know you too.

WHAT I MEANT TO SAY

I don't remember the exact words
I said to you, but I do remember
how they tasted bitter
and unforgiving, and
what I really meant to say,
was that you were always lovely,
even as you were walking away.

THE HARVEST

I still clip his spine in the spring,
when I till my garden
and feed my roses.

LET OLD BONES LIE

I never could tell
if it was my body
or my mind
he ached to strip.

He had a weakness
for pretty disasters
and ugly tragedies.
The cut
of his tongue
sliced through both.

Colors exploded
into me, violent
shades of him,
striking my soul.

Hush
your quaking
heart,
we have many
things to see.

Calling
rings hollow now
on the heels
of those
violent bells.

Let old bones
lie, I will
cut you
fresh roses.

Draw the cold
from my bones
and break me,
again. He was
the sweetest
regret I ever had
to swallow.

HEAVY HANDS

I used to wonder how
I could love him;
but he crept in slowly,
inch by careful inch
until he no longer reeked
of her and the kids he
never really wanted anyway.
But his hands grew heavy
until they left hints of him
behind, and I became the one
who reeked of dirty things
and wondered how anyone
could ever love me.

CHAPTERS OF US

I want to love you better.
Instead I will sign my name
to the words I have thrown
and the endings you have
written without me,
and maybe that will last
longer than this cold
and dark aching that breaks
along my spine each time
we begin another chapter of us.
No one says I love you
quite as beautifully
as the way you don't.

GUTTING THE APARTMENT UPSTAIRS

From time to time,
the sun will set hot
on my memories
and leave the cooling
to a breeze that swings
by my house and kicks
my front door down
just to tickle my lips
and call us square,
but I bite my lip
when I stand in line,
self serving at a checkout,
juggling multiple screws
and my home improvement,
and always wondering
if I should go back
and thumb through
the racks of red
swatches named so sweetly
as 'cherry', 'blush', and 'love',
by someone who has never
tasted passion, or love, or us,
or the way I thought love
should taste when it rolled off
of your tongue and poured
into my mouth before I inhaled
my smirk and swallowed the lies
of everyone here who has
lined up before me.

TWENTY EIGHTEEN

I want to love harder and hotter
than I ever have before,
and I want it to bend me in passion
until winter breaks into spring.
I want to find inspiration along roads
I have never thought to travel,
and I want to feel peace in the waters
I have never waded in.
I want to feel the pulse of cities
I have never set foot in,
and hear the stories of
strangers on a Wednesday afternoon.
I want to see beauty in eyes
that have never looked into mine,
and smell the colour
green on a rainforest floor.
I want to run faster than
my body has ever had to run,
and catch spring as she is
winking her way into summer.
I want to carry love in my hands
until they are overflowing
and place it in the hearts
I have broken before.
I want to climb
until I can climb no higher,
and feel summer give way
and surrender to fall.
I want to hear laughter and love
mixed with leaves crunching,
and I want to light fires
in our hearts to warm our winter souls.

BLOSSOM AND BONE

I am blossom and bone
with a soul on fire,
and I yearn to touch
the flesh and steel
of icy minds
with hearts willing to burn.

THE CURVE OF HER WISH

Perception is a tricky thing.
Sometimes what she believes
to be real is nothing more
than the sound lonely wishes make
when she has wrapped them
in defeat and set them loose
into a thirsty world.
And in those moments,
when I am picking her up
off the floor again, I wipe her
eyes and tell her there is nothing
wrong with a love built for speed
and something poetic about a woman
built for broken hearts.

CLUSTERS

It is as if some sort of cosmic energy
is continually pulsing through my veins,
cascading along, dancing with
my white blood cells, finding
a home in every organ of my body.
I hold the universe inside of me,
and I delight in the idea of that for days,
but when I hit blackest of holes, the galaxies
that live beneath my skin never cease.
Bone deep exhaustion near cripples me,
the melancholy swallows me alive,
but still, the stars erupt with every
ba-bump of my heartbeat, and shoot
through my system.
This world is a cruel place for a mad girl
with stars falling under her skin.

MIDNIGHT MIND

It's midnight in my mind again;
my thoughts are burning
and bursting like shooting stars.
Every breath is a bullet exploding
behind my eyes and dropping
bits of wishes down the back
of my neck, to die, and dying
itches, between my shoulder blades,
in that spot I can never quite reach.

A ROAD LESS TRAVELLED

I walk softly around the edge of it.
I am afraid to breathe.
My fingernails cut a path through
my palms and I exhale slowly,
watching the mantras I have pulled
from my blood, pooling in my hands.
I lift my fists to my lips
and I place the chant on my tongue,
loud enough to drown the song in my head
and flush the insanity from my ears.
Oh, to watch words fall like stars
and glow at my feet.

One step, two step
tippy tap, blue step
Blue step? two-step!
Click your heels, new step.
New step? Fool step!
Cut your teeth through step.

This is the place where I have come undone,
and I walk softly around the edge of it.
I whisper quietly in this place,
to this place, that seeps
into my brain and swallows my light.
From a distance this place looks like home
and I am weary again, a restless traveller.
I am starved for sleep, and in desperate need
of a place to hang my hat and rest my feet;
the two left feet that are weak at the knees
and stomp neon words into grains of sand
before they tip tap tippy-toe their way
to the fork in the road and leave
the dancing to the lucky ones
who are just passing through.

IN CRIMSON SCREAMS

I wonder what a quiet mind,
full of light, would feel like;
and if my memories could grow
cold, or if you would turn hot,
outside of the whispers
in the shadows you have
only ever known as home.

Softly now, my darling,
darkness has withered
the walls of this place,
and it is heavy and it is hanging,
always dripping like rain.

Now here we are,
inside the keeping, again.
I have made our bed between
my secrets and your dreams.
Pay no mind to the echoes at night;
these halls have been painted
in crimson screams.

BOTTOMS UP

I drink to the ones
that can sit with their souls
and not wish for sleep
and the nightmares
it brings.

DISCHARGED

It was addicting,
the attempt
to lose myself
inside of all
the others, until
I chilled my bones
in the shadows
cast by stoic
backs and upturned
eyes that refused
to see me, sacrificing.

OF MANIACS AND MANICS

You understand words like,
empty, dry, and nothing
but you'll never know
what hollow feels like
because your mind
will never take you under.
It won't swallow the smile
from your daughter's face
before it ever reaches your eyes.
You understand words like,
full, vibrant, and ecstasy
but you'll never know
what euphoria feels like
when you walk, body hot
on a wet summer's day
into a cool room,
worlds colliding on your skin.
You call me crazy
because I feel everything,
but I feel sorry for you
because you don't.

IN THE END

I have known love
and I have known loss,
but in the end,
they both looked
a lot like you.

UP IN SMOKE

This summer has hidden my faults
and distorted my memories
for a chance at a cool ride
on a hot moment deep
in the middle of July.
And I suppose if the pain in my back
and the ache in my bones
could be blamed on the weather,
then I would surely think that
the hopes I exhaled, into tiny slivers
during my sober minutes, had been
swallowed up in the wildfire smoke
that clings to the mountains,
hovers over my home, and sticks
in the fibres of my happy family.
And I would laugh when Mother
Nature spit them all out
in ashes, somewhere down south,
where BC smoke has been taxed
and inhaled as if it was gold.

UNDER RED SKIES

That night we smoked cigarettes
and talked of the red skies
that hung over us, above
right shoulders just East of town.
And although it was winter and chaos
danced with the blowing snow,
I felt the heat of those red skies.
It was somewhere inside of forty-five
mile an hour winds and the second
bottle of wine where I fell in love.

ON THE HIPS OF A HURRICANE

I could love you less
than storms or anything easy
that I have ever done,
but you, my hard love,
I love you as the moon
loves the tides, pulling
and pushing for one minute only,
for you to see that this life,
that our life, could be
extraordinary on the hips
of a hurricane or riding
the shoulders of a tropical storm.
You and I could devastate worlds,
the way we love each other,
churning and bursting inside
winds that will never kiss our lips.
You are my disaster,
and I will wait forever for you
to decide to ravage my shores.

IT IS WHAT IT IS

I loved him, as I once
loved you, but time
was not good to us
and love has never
been a friend of mine.

A SLIVER OF SILVER

I always made sure
our house was clean
even though we never were.
And I always made sure
the moon had a sliver to peer into,
a little slat between the pavement
and my pillow where she would feel
welcomed to lay her silver smile
upon our sleepless nights
and find us charmed enough
to dim her light when the sun came
to taunt us in the morning.
I am cleaner now,
than any porcelain corner
I spewed myself into,
but I still get high
off her manic energy when she tells me
she is happy to share,
because something is in the air
right now, in the full silver moon,
and I drink it all down as if it was my own.

ACID WASHED

He was downy soft
like summer mornings,
caught in the cuffs of jeans
that were knocked off hard
and rolled too tight.

CALL ME A GODDESS AGAIN

You could ruin Heaven
for me, the way you
keep worshipping my name.

STAR SONGS AND MOONLIGHT

You are my
deepest wishes,
a dark summer
sun blazing
sweet secrets
onto bronzed hips.
You are star
songs and moonlight
kisses I hide
under my shirt.

MUSE ME OR USE ME

Muse me, angel baby.
Ink me into bluish greys
and drop me in splashes.
Let me run, and drip
down creamy pages.

WOULD YOU COME WHEN I CALLED?

If I asked you for a kiss,
to breathe in the fire of me,
would you hold your breath
and singe your tongue?
If I asked you to walk
through mountains of ash
and sift the grains of love
out of my own destruction,
would you make your hands
work like shovels and fill
your heart like buckets?
If I asked you to sit
with me under cool moonlight
and tell me all the ways
you have been left unloved,
would you shudder from the cold
confessions you whispered
or writhe from the heat
of knowing you are loved?
If I ask you to leave
this God-awful place and make
a home from the waves
of the heartache we would create,
would you come when I called
and flood the world with our love?

FEEDING TIME

I know, she is beautiful;
all hot breath and pretty words,
but she has starved her demons
for a lifetime now,
and those motherfuckers are hungry.

HER WILD

They say she is too much
to handle, but when the moon
pulls the tide and the wolves
howl her name, blessed
are the ones who have been
taken by her wild.

A LIFETIME LEASE

I have swallowed oceans of doubt
and climbed mountains of shame,
but the ones who never loved me
have made their home inside my veins.

TWISTED SINS

I taste shame when I look
upon this table of cheaters
and whores, no better than me.
But I am the sheep
that wears the dirtiest cloak.
For it is dark and black as night,
made up of all things found
on the wrong side of the tracks.
The spot where sins twist
and dirty souls are shaped.
Somewhere along that midnight road,
between churches and graves,
you'll find my stolen spirit
and you're welcome to it.

HAUNTED

When did they become haunted,
these eyes of mine?
When the echoes of promises
tied the illusions of happiness
into knots in my hair and pulled
so hard, the frown in the corner
of my mouth was a sickening smile
when it settled into the whites
of my blind eyes.

STILL HAUNTED

Something dark followed me home
one night, it took up arms
and laid itself down in my soul.

I DON'T WANT YOU

I don't want you to leave them,
and forsake your twisted mind.
I don't want you to love me,
and have to leave your vultures behind.
I just want to sit in the light
your soul can't help but shine,
and I want to love you
as if you have always been mine.

FUCK YOU, DARLING

Forgive me, darling.
I still struggle
to put you into words;
how ridiculously arrogant of me.
To think I could ever hope
to grace this world with your light
when all I have to give is empty
lines and a devastated heart.
Fuck you, darling, for taking
my soul when you left.

THE COLOUR OF US

Water is wet and grass is green
and we are us, until it isn't
and we aren't, anymore.
And that's how it was, he and I,
right from the start: peas and carrots,
sand and surf, heaven and hell.
We were the late night phone calls
that went straight to voicemail,
the last light in the window
when all other doors were locked.
We were voracious laughter
muffling horrified screams.
We were bodies twisted in ecstasy
and minds broken in angst.
We were psych stays and breakdowns,
pills popped and death threats,
sirens wailing and holding cells.
We were life, on a September morning,
and death on an April night,
and in our own minds we were golden.

PANDERING

Sometimes I feel as if
I am pandering to savages,
sealing my soul and selling it
for an innocent kiss
or a quick fix.
And then I push and I shove,
and I make my way
to the front of the line
to buy it all back
from the wasted souls
who look an awful lot like me

WALKING WITH ANGELS

She peddled her promises,
and a story so sad,
I gathered angels
to sing her praises.
Even the devil
took a beat
to cock his head
and listen in admiration.
But a hook that high,
blazing through the night,
could never bring down the sun,
so I shrugged my shoulders
and the devil laughed
when I walked my angels home.

A SHARP LEFT TURN

I dig sharp left turns
on sunny mornings
and avoiding calls
on lazy days.
I dig a quick trip
to a dirty corner
store to grab ice
for drinks served
at community dinners
where angry diners
are full of shit
and good conversation.
I dig long lost love
and the letters never sent,
and anyone who would
leave a message in a bottle.

ELIXIR

As of today, I have gone
five days without drinking
a cup of coffee,
and the state of the world
would be alarming right now
if I wasn't so hell-bent
on this caffeine-free suicide.
But I see the world,
through clearer eyes now,
as some sort of self
involved expert.
I am almost a week
without stimulants,
so that has to make me divine.
And in my divinity,
I have noticed that
some people age well,
they wear their years
like ballroom dresses,
but I have yet to find
the elixir that scrubs
the years from my eyes.
I have lived as I have loved,
and I have loved well and hard,
and there is something about
the beauty of it all
that settles in the wrinkles
below my eyes and the creases
on my forehead that makes me think
I would be striking in a gown of my own.

TO DRINK AND TO SEE YOU, AGAIN

Do I need to drink
to see you again,
cut myself open
again, to bleed
you out in a rush?
You're gone now,
packed up and left
again, always fucking
again, until again
means nothing unless
I drink and I drug,
again, and I split
the cosmos, again.
Until I scream louder,
again, and faster than
the stars can carry you.
Until I can cry again,
until the edge
of the world comes
bursting again, so I can
come bursting again,
and then meet you, sliced
open again, somewhere
where blood no longer bleeds
red and you no longer leave,
again.

CUT OFF

"I love you"
had never sounded quite as bitter
until I heard it pouring from your mouth,
mixed with red wine.
"I loved you"
had never looked quite like scripture
until I watched it swirling in the water
against the stains you left behind.

MISUNDERSTOOD

When I told you that
I had been broken
before; it wasn't
a fucking challenge.

REMEMBER THIS

I will unwrap all of me
and lay myself naked
at your door,
but remember this:
I will bite back.
With every promise
you have broken
and every lie
you have told,
I will bite back.
But if you would meet me,
naked and aching,
I would give back every promise
I have broken
and swallow every lie
I have told.
I would give back,
everything I have sworn
and the little I have left,
to the one brave enough
to bare their filthy soul
next to mine.

BENEATH GOD AND SUNSHINE

I still keep you here, buried
beneath god and sunshine,
hidden in the happy places
I have long since forgotten.
But the taste of you here,
smothered under my breath,
rolls in my stomach like the
sad songs we never danced to,
and every sweat-soaked regret
that walked me home at dawn.
And still, I keep you here,
hidden, while you keep
turning my stomach,
and fighting to jump
from the tip of my tongue.

LITTLE DEATHS

There are little deaths
in every bit of remembering,
and all of the forgetting.
The truth is I don't know
if I should bleed for you,
or for me.

BUT YOU WERE

Not all prisons
have locks
not all secrets
are sacred
but you
were
midnight whispers
trapped inside
twisted minds
and heavy hearts

MIDNIGHT CRAVINGS

I crave nothing in this life
like I crave forgiveness.
I practice rolling it around
my mouth, bouncing it off
my cheeks, and tucking it
beneath my tongue, just
in case I ever have a right
to taste it.

MUSIC TO MY EARS

I have always loved the sound
of worlds bursting,
and other people falling in love.
I have always found something
beautiful that breaks wide open
in the midst of stars dying
inside pleading eyes;
something that screams above
the intensity of souls colliding
with other souls not quite
as lovely as my own.

FAUCETS TO WEST

I am not a good woman.
I am sons upon light years,
daughters making hard love
with blue moons and every
wish on every fallen star
cast forth through double-panes
on lonely Friday nights
like the ones you swore you would
never relive again.
I am not a good woman.
I tuck my dreams in at night now,
behind balconies not yet barred
until our youngest heart decides
she is not yet a good woman
and scales the walls we have built
to keep her in and safe, and completely
ignorant and pure.
I am not a good woman.
But I am here still, hiding
in the bushes on the corner of our
1/4 acre dream lot,
the dream yard
of the dream home
we have signed our souls away for.
I am not a good woman.
And every time I turn faucets west
and soak the morning in glory
I am met with caws and crass reminders
that no matter how much water
I pour upon this place,
there is a fire smouldering in the ditch
and though I am not a good woman,

I would watch, unliving and unloved,
and I would lay it all down and weep
my tears will never be enough
to ever see our name
on a green sign, that marks our home.

IN THOSE MOMENTS

I liked to sit with her
in those moments,
when night gave way
to dawn, and she would
wash her face,
and peel herself out
of last night's fantasies.
I rubbed the miles
from her feet
and she would tell me
heavy stories until
we laughed, and she said
it was time to go home.

BEFORE HIM

I locked my hands around her wrists
and I held on for dear life while I watched her,
that wildling spirit, pull the thunder
from the sky and place it in our veins.

DURING HIM

Darling, don't ever doubt me.
I will climb down your throat
and beat his fists until they
are bloody and you are angry
enough to spit them out
and breathe right again.

AFTER HIM

It's not him, she said,
when I rubbed my thumb
across her cheek, pushing
the red into the green
like two lost lovers
screaming in pain.
I wondered why she wished
he had never left, when
in that moment I told her
everything would be okay,
and gone had never felt so close.
I pulled the drapes against the heavy dawn
and I drew her wet eyes down
to cover the words that still hung
from the corners of her mouth.

IT'S TIME TO GO HOME

I see you there weeping
on the stairs unable to climb
another yet too afraid to descend.
And I know the bags you have
packed and placed at your feet
are far heavier than they were
when you came here.
Unrequited love sits funny
inside luggage, it takes up space
meant for happier memories
and until you climb on top and let
the weight of your heavy heart
fiddle with the zipper,
you'll wander aimlessly,
always searching for the spot
where you feel safe enough
to unpack your baggage.

THE TROUBLE WITH HEARTS

This evening I woke
to the sound of Spring
banging her fists,
full of blossoms,
against my front door,
and I wondered how
long it has been
since you smelled
anything other than deep
earth and the absence
of rotting love.
I still wake up,
strung out and smelling
you on my skin,
thinking the dead
should always be left
with their hearts.
Pin mine to my
dress and leave me
to rot, it has loved too
hard to burn.

AGAIN, DARLING

I have torn my wings
again, darling
and the blisters are raw
on my feet,
but I will meet you deep
in the woods with nothing
more than a cold heart
and a fiery soul.
I have been watching clocks
again, darling
and how flowers bloom
the way seasons die,
and I have been waiting for you.

WE'RE ALL A LITTLE ILLITERATE

We wear poems on our skin;
those words were carved
into our bones when we were
born into a world sadly
lacking good poetry, and far
too filled with shame to ever
let us dance naked, and swing
our stories from our hips.

INKED

I carved you deep.
Your words on my mind,
your name into my skin.

FREE BIRDS

We wore the wind
like wings and turned
our eyes toward the sky.

WISH FOR ME

Never send me red roses
tied with perfect red ribbons
and a note that says you have missed me.
Instead come to my door
with your hands full of stems
and tell me that you have wished for me.

LET IT GO

There are tides
that will always turn
and hearts that will
forever change,
but something beautiful
happens when nothing
ever stays the same.

LONELY ROADS AND DEAD ENDS

I know you're hurting,
and I know you've been busy
pulling the shards of your heart
from the tips of Cupid's arrows,
but I promise you,
it was still love.
Sometimes love splinters
and it cracks the foundation
of every which way you have
never had to travel, until now,
and though the road will be long
and twisted into dead ends,
you'll eventually make it home,
and you will love again.

You will love again.

TAKING UP SPACE

I may never see you.
I may never be able to play
with your hair because
your head may never be in my lap,
and I may never breathe
the same air, in the same place,
at the same time as you,
but just knowing that you're here,
taking up space on the same realm
as I am, gives me comfort.
Don't you dare try to go
before our time is up,
I need you here,
for purely selfish reasons.

THE WORLD WILL FIGHT

I have tasted the pain
between grief and love
far too many times to expect
a young soul like yours
to navigate its way through
life without my lessons.
So here I am, an old soul,
eating pain and swallowing love
so you can live inside brighter days
always shining on the horizon,
and you will know that even galaxies
burst beautifully under pain
great enough to build something
endless from your tears, something
the world would fight to carry.

LIKE NEW

It all comes out
in the wash.
Get in the water,
my love, things
are never quite
as dirty as they seem.

MOVE ME

Sever my roots,
and push me
from this cloud
dreamer of dreams;
my soul needs
to breath, my spirit
needs to stretch
her wings.

STOIC

I will not force
a pretty smile
upon my face
to please eyes
that no longer
see me.

LUNA

They talk of their landings
and her dust, and they watch
her world swallow miracles,
even on the darkest nights,
when she cloaks herself
to play with simple men.
We still call her down,
in stones and prophesies,
on the chants of our sisters,
when we find our place
in the waves, and her in our blood,
and we know for certain
that this, that she, is how
legends have always been born.

IT ALL MAKES SENSE

I understand now,
how she could be
everything to a heart
that valued nothing.

WAR DOGS AND WISHES

I fight a war within
myself that I am certain
will leave me with casualties.
I struggle to hold on to
what little I have left
before it all turns to haze
and vanishes forever.
But I also start fires
to burn memories
and I fan the flames
and I urge those fires on
and into no more.
I fight a war within
myself that I am certain
will leave me with casualties,
but perhaps the gods of war
will take pity on them, and I
will finally lay them to rest.

FUCKING HEARTS

Every fucking night
I wrestle the pieces
of my heart back out
of your bloody fucking
hands, and then I wake,
bleeding from my chest
and spend my day wondering
why the good girls always
make their beds inside
the bad boys fucking hearts.

BATTLE CRIES BLARING

Cry. Scream. Give the world
your fucking worst, it wont go
easy on any of us, but you
best get your ass back up
off the ground with
your battle cries blaring.
You are a goddamn warrior
and even warriors have moments
when they question their worth,
go ahead and question it, but do it
quickly, the rest of us fledglings
are waiting on you with battle
cries scratching our throats,
and trails ready to burn.

LUNA'S DAUGHTER

She is the sway of the waves
being pulled by the moon.
She is the sorrow in the goodbye
when life ended too soon.
She is but once in a lifetime
and far too many times before.
She is something that just happens,
and she is everything worth waiting for.

IT'S ONLY POETRY

If they ask how I was able to turn
pain into beauty and bring
their darkness to the light,
tell them it was only poetry.
Don't tell them how your name
still swirled under my tongue
no matter how many times
I fought to swallow it.
Don't tell them about the nights
I spent locked inside my mind
and how bitter charcoal
was the only thing to save me.
Don't tell them how I wore
the darkest parts of the night
and walked hand-in-hand
with demons and insomnia.
Don't tell them how I plucked
the stars from weeping eyes
and tried to barter them
for wishes and some sleep.
Don't tell them how I lived
between the darkness and the light,
just tell them I lived with poetry
tucked beneath my skin.

ACKNOWLEDGMENTS

As always, first and foremost, I must acknowledge and give thanks to my husband Scott, and our brilliant daughters, Brinly and Tatym, for always understanding why I must retreat into myself in order to push the devils out of me and bleed them onto paper. I am always stunned, and ever so grateful, to find them happily waiting, and beaming with pride, when I resurface again.

A huge thank you, and a big shout out, to the badass writers who read an advance copy of Blossom and Bone and dug it enough to write some pretty wicked reviews. I tell you, there is nothing in this world that compares to the feeling you get when a writer you have admired for so long not only reads your book, but also lends their name and their thoughts to the pages inside. Yeah, I'm still fangirling over here because of you: Samuel Decker Thompson, Nicholas Gagnier, Liz Newman, and Candice Louisa Daquin, thank you all so much.

Thank you to Mitch Green, the wicked designer who has created the stunning covers of not only this book, but WORLD as well. Thank you for always turning my mess of documents and scraps of barely legible emails into something beautiful. I have been fortunate and blessed to work with you and I can't wait to see what else you and I can create. You are the kindness and most talented badass book designer I know. It's always a pleasure and an honour to carry your name and feature your work with mine.

To Candice Daquin, my darling poetess and champion of all that is good and right in this world, I am forever indebted to you. Your words about my words are something I am never quite prepared for, and that you would honour me with the beauty of your words, as the foreword to this book is a gift beyond any I have ever received. I am truly in awe of you, as a writer, as a woman, and as an outstanding example of the kind of person I hope to one day become. I love you, and I thank you again. To Christine E. Ray, my editor, my peer, my friend, I stand in awe and the warmth of your light. With the deepest respect and the utmost love, I thank you. I thank you for taking on the chore of editing this book, and for setting me right every single time I tried to go left. And above everything else, I thank you for your love and your fierce dedication to our collective, and every member who is blessed to work with you. Thank you for keeping SD on the rails when we train wrecks so often burst into flames, that you for keeping us on track and putting out our fires. And thank you for gracing us all with your art; you are the queen badass of us all.

To my peers and my friends, Miss Georgia Park, Nicholas Gagnier, Matthew D Eayre, Alfa Holden, Stephanie Bennett-Henry, Kindra M Austin - thank you for always supporting me and for sharing your art with us all.

Jasper, Thank you for always having my back, I hope you know I've always got you.

ABOUT THE AUTHOR

Nicole Lyons is a tornado harnessed into the body of a writer, social activist, voice for the downtrodden, and a powerful poet whose words reveal truth like a scalpel through silk. A Consulting Editor and long-time member of the Sudden Denouement Literary Collective, her writing is featured in *Anthology Volume I: Writings from the Sudden Denouement Literary Collective.*

Lyons' essays, articles, and poetry can be found in The Mighty, The OCH Literary Society, Anti-Heroin Chic, Sidereal Catalyst, and OTV Magazine. She was inducted into The Mental Health Writer's Guild in 2015 for her work on The Lithium Chronicles, Psych Central, The Mighty, and the International Bipolar Foundation. Lyons volunteers as a speaker and event coordinator with a Canadian non-profit that focuses on suicide awareness and prevention in children and teens.

The best-selling author of *HUSH* (no longer in print) and *I am a World of Uncertainties Disguised as a Girl* (Sudden Denouement Publishing) lives a good life in beautiful British Columbia with her daughters and husband. From her sunny porch, Lyons is enjoying a glass of wine, and working on her much anticipated fourth collection of poetry.